The Seven Habits
of Happily
Retired People

The Seven Habits of Happily Retired People

*A Guide to Living
a Cheerful Retirement*

DENNIS C. BREWER

First Edition

Printed in the United States of America

ISBN-13: 978-0-9795559-2-3
ISBN-10:   0-9795559-2-2

This text is dedicated to my grandchildren and step-grandchildren who are growing up in a time where both living the American Dream and the notion of retiring financially well-off in their 60s is becoming an increasingly elusive goal for far too many people.

"Whatever it might be that is keeping you separated from reaching out and achieving a greater level of happiness, set that aside now and evaluate your ability to grasp all or at least some of the seven habits of happily retired people and hold them as your own."

—Dennis C. Brewer

About the Author

Dennis C. Brewer was born in Michigan's Upper Peninsula and is a graduate of Michigan Technological University, from which he holds a Bachelor of Science Degree in Business Administration. He is a veteran of military service to the United States of America that includes enlisted service in the Navy and commissioned officer service in the Army Reserve and the Michigan Army National Guard. His varied career path includes experience in military, state and federal government, private enterprise, and in his consulting practice. Travel to Japan, Taiwan, China, Hong Kong, England, Canada, Germany, and the Philippines contribute to his world view and humanitarian perspectives. Dennis has many nationally published books and articles included in his writing credits. He and his wife, Penny, are currently traveling the United States and living in their Fleetwood Terra LX motor home with a goal of visiting interesting areas and places of interest in all of the lower 48 states.

Contents

Contents

Foreword

My friendship with Dennis Brewer began in our kindergarten classroom in 1955. I will always remember this red-headed boy because we continued moving up the grades of our elementary school and on to middle school then on to high school together. Dennis and I had last names that began with the letter B so we were frequently seated near one another as youngsters for all those years while in school. Dennis as I recall, was a quiet, sweet boy during our school years together. I remember him as a bit serious in high school sitting there in his ROTC uniform and, for some odd reason; I remember that Dennis wore motorcycle type boots on the days that he wasn't in his uniform. I guess back then this quiet kid had an edge, but he was not the "Fonzie" type at all. He certainly never passed me a note or shot a spit ball at me, which was the thing to do to get attention in study hall!

After high school, Dennis and I went our separate ways to marry and raise our families, both of us experiencing military life that took us off to see the world far away from our small home town. When I reunited with Dennis it was 40 plus years later at our class reunion, and I recognized him right away. We had a nice conversation, and I learned that he was retired, like my husband Jack, and planning for this new chapter in his life. I was so thrilled to hear that he had written and published several books, and I was so proud of him! I also was very surprised and excited to hear that he married our mutual childhood friend Penny, too! They apparently shared a love of motorcycles back in the '60s, I was told but I don't ever remember Penny with any motorcycle gear on back then! How cool, I thought, that they both had been so adventurous! Since our reunion, Dennis, Penny, and I have renewed our friendship and had fun reminiscing about the good old days of growing up in our small Upper Peninsula Michigan town and sharing what those years in between brought us to today. I also realized that Dennis and I were in the same class once again! Kids of the '60s, in our 60s, and RETIRED! Although I joked that my husband Jack was retired but that I was merely TIRED! I was tired but trying to figure out what to do with all the time we suddenly had on our hands. Dennis and Penny, though, had their retirement all figured out it seemed. They told us of their plans to sell their home and to simplify their lives by ridding themselves of a lot of their stuff! They also said that they were going to buy a large motor home to travel the country in and use it as their home. I was reminded that these two continued to have that adventurous spirit of the motorcycle-riding teenagers that they once were! I admired how eager Dennis and Penny were to try a new way of living while retired.

I had dedicated my life to my husband and our three kids and helped to raise a grandson. It was a very busy time for me. We built a big house, and we lived the American Dream. Suddenly, it seemed, the house was quiet, and my job was over! All at once, it seemed, it was only Jack, myself, and our dog, Buddy, staring at the walls and looking out at our big backyard with the swings sitting still. Our kids and grandkids all lived close by, but they had their own busy lives and big backyards. So "What now?" Do I enjoy this peace and quiet that I dreamed about and looked forward to when I was overwhelmed during my mommy years? I was so accustomed to giving to my family and putting my needs aside that I really felt like a fish out of water. Out of boredom, I took on a part-time job, working in a showroom for a kitchen cabinet maker for something to do with all this spare time. I loved the opportunity to play with my passion for design that I toyed with as a home-maker. What Jack and I realized, though, was that my new job cramped our new style as retirees because I was tied down again and we couldn't take off on a fun trip on a whim! I soon gave up the idea of being tied down with a job, so it didn't last long. We took several trips to Mexico and a few road trips throughout the country these past several years, but we still had this big house and were con-stant slaves to our huge yard! I can see now that we didn't plan our retirement very well. Well, to be honest, we had just been winging it! When I heard from Dennis that he was writing a book about living a happy retirement life, I couldn't wait to read it! After reading it, I can tell you that I'm excited to put Dennis's book, *The Seven Habits of*

Foreword

Happily Retired People, and its great guide into play while
in our retirement years. I'm looking forward to freeing
myself of this big house and much of the accumulated
stuff (be it tangible or mental baggage), going on to this
next chapter of our life with more confidence, and living a
happier existence! Taking the steps that Dennis outlines so
brilliantly in his book into play in our life is a wonderful
gift to me from that little red-headed boy who sat next to
me in elementary school. I'm so proud of him, my friend,
and I am so honored to have been asked to write a foreword for this book. He has done an incredible job of creating a guide to a cheerful retirement life for you, the reader.

It will be obvious to you that Dennis C. Brewer has
thoroughly studied what to cover while writing *The Seven
Habits of Happily Retired People*. Believe me, I know that
he walks the talk, too! *The Seven Habits of Happily Retired
People* outlined in his book are such a gift to anyone planning to retire. Also, it is a great book for those of us who
would like to experience most happily this next chapter of
our "Baby Boomer" lives. You will find that this guide all
makes sense for achieving the most rewarding retirement
experience.

Barbara Bayles King
Redmond, Washington

Preface

I count myself as one very fortunate lower-middle-class baby boomer. I say that because, during my work life, I was never bored with work and managed to have multiple successful job positions, some by choice, and others quite by chance. My work experience includes grease monkey, bread truck driver, electrician, loan officer, enlisted USN sailor, office manager, commissioned USA engineer officer, network administrator, information technology solutions specialist, consultant and, last but not least, state park maintenance attendant.

Through all of that, I dabbled in a business or two, performed occasional technology consulting services, and wrote a few books. The work was never boring, but it was all, each and every job, real hard work. From my very first job, I planted in my head the idea that someday I would not work and would retire to live out my remaining years. I thought I might have to retire, be medically retired, or perhaps just want to retire. For me, it ultimately became the latter. Although the income at first would be very slim, a 72 percent reduction in income, I found myself in a position where I wanted to retire, and it was possible. So it was that at age 56 I voluntarily put in my retirement papers and bid adieu to the everyday world of work.

Once you retire, you may find, as I did, that you get to spend time, sometimes a lot of time, with other retirees. Once in retirement status, I quickly learned that not all retired persons are happy. In fact, many of them are downright downers for themselves and for all who come into contact with them. They seem to have little clouds of doom and gloom hanging over their path. They are unhappy, and they let you know it, both by their behaviors and in their conversation. All the while, others I have met seemed to be genuinely enjoying everyday life, and they savor retirement. I set about to find out why some are so very happy, even content, and others are . . . well, sad, to be polite about it. I thought there might be a book idea in all of it once I figured it all out. At first, having to struggle a bit financially myself, I thought the abyss between happy and sad retired individuals and couples would be mostly about money or wealth. We are naturally cued into and inundated with commercials about the wealth needs for retirement, and I genuinely thought that would be the key factor. And, if not wealth, perhaps it is just financial sufficiency. However, over my six years of intense observation and interviewing, I found many examples where the wealth or appearance of it was there but the happiness was quite elusive. I also found enough instances where retired couples were quite content despite their very limited financial means and very modest lifestyles, that I began to doubt my assumption. Over time, I discovered that it was more about attitude toward money in retirement. More importantly, by doing the research and follow-on analytics, I discovered and reckoned out the seven primary habits observed and ingrained in the character and actions of the happiest of the retirees I had the privilege to meet. Those common characteristics became the subject areas of this book. Frank McKinney Hubbard (1868–1930), a noted American cartoonist and journalist, is attributed as having said something to the affect that: "It is pretty hard to tell what does bring happiness; poverty and wealth have both failed." From my humble perspective, Frank McKinney Hubbard was right on target with that idea; happiness comes as the result of the actions we choose to take this moment in this day. Well-honed habits help us take those daily actions, even when our preference in the moment might be to do nothing at all.

There may be many other habits generally associated with happily retired people; I am not so brazen as to assume that I captured them all in this text. If there are, my disclaimer is that I did not observe other behaviors a sufficient number of times to call it a common characteristic of the happy retirees I have had the honor to meet. I do know that the habits included in this book are shared, important, even dominant, and that the happiest retirees seem to own and display by their actions most, if not all, of these seven habits.

It is my hope that you find one or more of these habits useful to you in your own life and in your retirement for many years to come.

Introduction

This book is intended for those readers who are 50 or over and retired or soon-to-be retired. It is certainly OK to read this book long before retirement, but it is envisioned to be of most benefit to those who are retired by choice or by chance and are not totally satisfied currently with their daily life in retirement. After working for decades, retiring may be the biggest lifestyle adjustment you will encounter in your whole life. The transition is not always easy for everyone. This text is intended for those who have discovered, anticipate, or wonder if retirement is about more than having cash and capital assets or sufficient cash flows from savings, retirement checks, and/or investments. As you read this book, it is my hope that you will discover that a happy retirement is found by developing a retirement lifestyle that is centered on one's free expression of self—the freeing of the real person within who was previously trapped in the daily rigors of making a living, running a business, maintaining a home, or taking care of children and family matters.

Also I wish to be totally up front and tell you what this book is *not* about. This book is not about preparing mentally for retirement. There are plenty of other texts on that topic. It is not about fiscal or financial planning for retirement. It is not about capital preservation during retirement or making plans and accommodations for long-term care. This book is all about outlining meaningful lifestyle choices for yourself that appear to contribute substantially to a happy, fun-filled, and fulfilling retirement lifestyle.

Most of us look forward to our "golden years," when our time is really our own, but some people dread retirement. How will they fill all that time? Still others say they can't wait to retire, but, once they do, they're completely miserable. While the retired reader is encouraged to compare his or her current lifestyle habits with the concepts presented in this book, the soon-to-be-retired reader will find it useful for evaluating his or her readiness for the changes to come. Retirement is about letting go of both the stressful demands of work and giving up one's precious time in exchange for a pay check. It is a time to live life to its fullest potential. My hope is that reading this book will put you on the right track to reaching that potential.

It is said that repeating the same activity every day for 21 days makes a new habit. That means that, if you are on the wrong side of any of these life-living, retirement-enjoying habits, there is probably time to change your choices about how you spend your hours and days. Appreciate that every day that you are alive is an opportunity to make positive changes in your life. This is your chance to change old habits and old thinking that may be preventing you from finding a truly happy life in your retirement years. If you work fearlessly at making changes and relentlessly stay at it, you can make all seven habits your own in just 147 days. Forty percent of one year could bring you to a totally different outlook on this "new life." Now is the time to focus on yourself and begin practicing the habits that will lead to a fulfilling retirement.

Giving up on the working life is very hard for some people. Sometimes it's the money, at other times it is fear of becoming bored or being poor or both. For others it's an overwhelming feeling of self-importance summed up by self-examining questions like: "How could the world or this company live without my talent and daily contributions?" Whatever it might be that is keeping you separated from reaching out and achieving a greater level of happiness, set that aside now and evaluate your ability to grasp all or at least some of the *seven habits of happily retired people* and hold these habits as your own. To a great degree, achieving happiness in retirement is attitudinal, and only you can adjust your attitude. But know this—it is also actionable. That is, in order to make the attitude real to your conscious and subconscious, it must be acted out in some way each and every day. The hours of each day, if only filled with thoughts surrounding wanting something, will at the end of the day leave you tired and feeling miserable, possibly in deep despair. Contrarily, if positive thoughts are put into constructive actions, no matter how small each action may be, at the day's conclusion, you will be filled with a feeling of some magnitude of accomplishment. Even a day of total relaxation (doing nothing productive), when established as that day's only goal, is considered a success when it is achieved.

Consider how life was supposedly lived in primitive hunting and gathering societies. It typically took less than three hours a day for primitive men and women to provide food and clothing, and the rest of the day was available for socialization, helping others, creative endeavors, or recreating. Despite the changes that force us to live to rigid work-week schedules—thanks to the industrialized society we live in—our human anatomy and capacity for mental well-being is much better designed for the hunting and gathering lifestyle. A slower life, characterized by a methodic and measured pace instead of living on the cutting edge and being immersed in the "rat race," is programmed into our DNA. Unlike many other creatures on this planet, we were designed for minimal work and maximum relaxation. Culture has provided the push-push of getting more, the working harder to get ahead ethic, and the whole myth that everything has to be competitive and there must be winners and losers in all aspects of our public and private lives.

Regrettably, too much of this competitive force is carried over into our private and family lives. Carrying over into retirement that "rat race thinking" can ruin anyone's retirement. Retirement is a time intended for each of us to get into our inner selves and away from the false construct that we are valueless without paid work: it is a time to reclaim the lifestyle we are naturally programmed to live. Those who are able to find their inner selves during retirement and do what makes them happy regardless of the opinions and judgments of others are the ones who adjust to and enjoy life as a retired person.

My hope is that as you read this book you will do some self-examination and look into your inner self to find the gold nuggets within that will bring you ever closer to a happy and fulfilling life in retirement. Whether you have a day left to live or grace will grant you 50 more years, you are entitled to find and release the nascent inner self who wishes for the opportunity to express itself in positive ways during your retirement years.

When I told a few of my close associates that I was writing a book about what it takes to live a contented retirement, their first question was: "What are your credentials for writing on that topic?" It is funny that I never heard that question from anyone regarding my more technical books. The assumption apparently was that I knew enough about the technical topics to pontificate on them and that I knew little or nothing about life in retirement. It occurred to me that readers of this book might harbor the same question. The answer is a simple one. Although my retirement began at age 56, my planning for retirement began at age 16. Not only have I had the vision of my retirement since I was a young man, I have been practicing and creating that vision since January of 2006. So I can claim eight years of experience—more than enough experience based on time for licensure in most trades.

The early goals were twofold. The first was financial freedom apart from any semblance of having to punch a clock for someone else. The second and equally important goal was the freedom itself that retirement offers. The freedom to do, see, hear, smell, and taste, to touch and feel the new and different along with the familiar and exotic; to experience the best of life in this body. Pursue other fleeting interests that did not necessarily have a financial gain component, such as freedom to travel and spend time writing, were important to me as I looked toward my retirement.

Over the course of my working life, as I planned to create my vision, I read everything I came across about retirement, so I am sure I have been influenced a bit by all of the magazine articles and books I have ever read on the topic. All of those studied topics, however, were on the nuts and bolts, dollars and cents of retiring, leaving me with a huge gap in understanding about actually living a quality and fulfilling lifestyle while retired. This book is an attempt to fill that knowledge and experience gap for others.

The other retirement expertise credential that I bring to the table is in the power and value of lifelong observations of those around me and critical analysis of those observations. The learning value of never-ending observations of other people living their lives provides a tuition-free course in human behaviors. Watching others go about their everyday lives, living out the human condition is indeed its own laboratory for those willing to observe and thoughtfully process what is being seen and heard. The experts on retirement that I "consulted with" were countless other already-retired people. Some were "experts" on how to be happy, and an equal number were "experts" on how to be totally unhappy in retirement. The examples were all around me all of my life, and I expect they are around you, too. When you see an older couple in a restaurant who only speak to the waitress and never to each other during the full course of their meal, there is a lesson here. Has that ever happened to you while dining out? When acquaintances of yours who are retired constantly bicker at each other, and one spouse works hard at belittling the other, there is a lesson here, too. When retired couples find more ways to spend time with their individual "friends" than each other, there is a lesson to be learned from that also. When one spouse cannot even imagine giving up work to be "bored" at home while the other spouse yearns for the freedom to travel, there is a lesson. This book is a compilation of the few necessary habits I have learned and observed as being associated with those people who appear to be happy and fulfilled in their retirement lifestyle.

Working past your personal "medically-good-through date" is also problematic when one spouse is nursing-home bound too soon before the other. Retirement goals and lifelong dreams shattered, forsaken, or postponed are common causes for finding one's self very unhappy in retirement. The examples leading to additional clues about a happy or unhappy retirement are equally apparent when coupled with a probing question advanced here or there. Fortunately, no one has been offended by my queries, and almost everyone I asked questions of was willing to share part of their life experience that made them appear to me to be happy in retirement.

From these two lifelong perspectives, this book's contents are derived. That said, be honest with yourself as you evaluate your level of happiness and your motives for buying and reading this book. You may already own the seven habits of happily retired people, you may own only a few of them, or you may possess none at all. These ideas are offered to help you formulate a retirement lifestyles that is right for you. It is by no means intended to be a substitute or alternative to seeking and getting professional help of any sort regarding your life choices and situations during retirement. If you feel you need help from a financial planner, psychologist, psychiatrist, physician, accountant, religious leader, or lawyer—by all means, seek help from qualified professionals that you trust and get the help you feel you need. Similarly, if the habits mentioned in this book seem like they might move you closer to a happier retirement, then they are yours to try and to use to your own benefit. Please remember that you are using these lifestyle ideas at your own risk and a happily retired lifestyle could follow. That is my wish for every reader: that you can find the ways to be happier and more fulfilled in your remaining retirement years.

Acknowledgments

Many thanks are due to all of the people who knowingly and unknowingly provided me with the ideas and concepts presented in this book by living parts of their lives before my eyes and ears. Without the many positive examples of people who appear genuinely happy in retirement, this book would not have been possible. Regrettably, perhaps sadly, the same thanks are due to the countless examples of those who appear to be living an unhappy or "dead-end" retirement. It saddens me to think of the negative examples, even though thanks are due to them, for it was this group that provided the motivation to capture the good examples into this simple text. If one person or a hundred benefit from reading this book by increasing their happiness and pleasure in their own retirement, much credit is due to those who provided the examples in their own lives. I can only take credit for putting the life examples into a text that can be shared with the world of readers.

I would like to thank everyone who played a role in the development of this book. To all of you who were retired and met me in the last eight years or so, odds are you played a role in helping me confirm the ideas presented here by your example. I would like to thank my

Acknowledgments

wife, Penny, for granting me some of our time together so that this project and many of my other writing projects can be completed. Many thanks to my friend Barbara for taking the time to write the foreword for this book. Thank you to Patricia Wallenburg of TypeWriting for a great job with the layout. Thank you Annie Woy of Blue Moon Editorial Services for copy editing.

CHAPTER 1

Using Available Financial Resources

You may have consumed almost all of your life's energy up to this point stockpiling money, possessions, food, real estate, and furnishings; investing in stocks and bonds; and acquiring collectibles of all sorts. You may be a millionaire, billionaire, or just an average middle-class guy or gal looking forward to retirement checks from a generous employer or simply someone looking forward to your very first social security check. Certainly, your financial status will impact the quality of the things and services that will be a part of your retirement, but wealth alone will not make your retirement years happy years. You can actually live a happy and rewarding retirement on a constrained budget. I know this first-hand because, as I write this, I am 64 and am already into my eighth year of a retirement that began on a single humble public employee's pension. The viewpoints, guidance, and commentary in this book are not coming from the millionaire next door. They are coming from a baby boomer of average means with a typical retirement income.

Some of the themes I have included in this book, I knew and embraced long before I retired. One I learned and embraced only this year. In addition, I always intuitively knew the axiom "Don't wait too long to retire." The horror stories from people waiting too long are boundless. You frequently hear about people who retire and then a major medical malady hits them and life changes permanently for the worse by being tied to nearby doctors and hospitals or being bound to the confines of a nursing home. Not as bad, but often frequently encountered, are those medical problems that prevent one from walking any distance, biking, or simply from being physically active at any level. There have been many published studies over the last few decades that demonstrate that early retirees who adjust well and early to a retirement lifestyle live longer, healthier, and happier lives.

A quality retirement is not normally possible without a regular source of disposable income. Retirement is not about getting more income or wealth; it is about using whatever financial resources you have to improve the quality of your life on a daily basis. The truth is, there may be no quality-filled tomorrows for you, but this is not a reason to panic about the future and continue to fret, keep working, and be a slave to saving for a "rainy day." There are always going to be unknowns and risks in your future, as there are in everyone's: knowing this should not prevent you from living your life to the fullest potential in the present. Your future is made from summing up all of the "what to do" and "done" in the next hour, over and over again.

Business planners frequently talk about having a strategic plan (for the distant future) and a tactical plan (for the present and near term). The reality for business and for a life lived fully is that where you will be two, five, or 10 years down the road will be fashioned from the sum of the results of how you spend your time and money each and every day right now. Your daily tactical activities are all milestones of what your strategic finish will be irrespective of what the "on paper" strategic plan or goals for the future might be.

The biblical quote comes to mind that "no man can serve two masters." You can focus your energy in your remaining years on keeping up the balances in your various investment accounts, or you can focus on using those balances to keep up with funding the life you wish to live today.

So let's delve right into the first and perhaps the most controversial habit for a happy life in retirement.

Happily Retired Habit #1

Guiltlessly spend 90 to 100 percent of your disposable annual income on yourself and your spouse or life partner.

The key words here are "guiltlessly" and "disposable." So what is meant by guiltlessly? To answer that question,

I present this experience from my own life. I was being advised about decision-making by a Navy Commander after I made the rank of Chief Petty Officer (CPO). It is said that CPOs run the ships and the Navy itself, and now I was in that exclusive club at a very young age. I suppose my youth motivated him to think I needed to be clued in on a few tips that he thought many of the old salts already knew. His council was to the effect that, as a CPO, I would be counseling the men and women in my charge; making decisions, disciplining, and even giving out family advice to the junior ranking and often younger sailors. He seemed to have not noticed that some of the men working for me had nearly more time in the Navy than I had years on the planet. Nonetheless, he thought everyone in the chain of command would look up to me for leadership and advice despite my youth at the time, and he felt I needed to be ready for it. He was the first of the many "one-minute" commanders and leaders I would run into during my 25 plus years in the military, both active and reserves, so he had to boil the lesson down to its core, knowing—or at least thinking—that if he had rattled on too long my eyes would roll back into my head. Well, he did "boil down" the lesson to a few simple phases. He first said, "When the sailors or spouses ask you a question, you are expected to have an answer." Next he said that when you know you have the workable answer from your own knowledge or experiences, share it without hesitation. When you don't have the answer, apply this test before you give a thought-out answer: simply ask if what you are about to suggest, say, do, or act on: "Is it Legal? Is it moral? Is it just?" If the answer to all three is yes, then proceed without any reluctance. In those rare instances where the only answer you can think of will not pass this acid test of legal, moral, and just, then ask, "Will it save a life?" If so proceed. If not, do nothing, say nothing, and perhaps time will bring the right answer. What he was saying, essentially, was to make decisions, and to encourage others to make decisions, that will serve to completely eliminate the possibility of guilt.

Often, spending money to actually enjoy retirement or agreeing to spend money is the biggest struggle that many retired couples face. Thoughts that begin with "I feel bad if I spend money on..." or "I don't deserve it" are negative, self-defeating feelings and should be blocked out. You should never feel bad if you make an adult decision to spend your own resources on anything that is based on an ethical standard that involves behaviors or actions that are legal, moral, and just. As a retiree, you deserve to enjoy any of the activities and actions that you can afford on your available cash flow and that meet your personal standard of ethical behavior. Behaviors that will not harm you or others are all on the table of possibilities. Traveling, making trips to the spa, getting a weekly massage, and acting to achieve all the check boxes on your bucket list are examples of things that you should be expending your financial resources on in your retirement years. You have a basic right to spend on things you enjoy. Regrettably, seniors get advice to the contrary from their spouses, off-spring, financial advisors, lawyers, and family members. Well-intended though they be, feel free to ignore them. Empower yourself to say "It is my money and I will spend it my way, but thank you for your advice. And, oh by the way, feel free to follow the advice you have offered to me in your own life. This one is mine, what is left of it—all mine—and I will decide what to do or not do with it." If you are spending your nest egg or retirement cash flows in a manner that is legal, moral, and just, then the chances for regret will be minimized if not eliminated entirely.

Retirement is about living your lifestyle to the limits of what your financial resources will allow—living what is left of your so-called "golden years" to the fullest every single day. Providence only knows the number of our days as an active participant in the physical and thoughtful activities on spaceship Earth. After age 55, being in retirement status is about using every one of those days, every minute of each day, to that day's best advantage.

At age 55, in the United States, common mortality tables shows 27 years left to live on average; at 65, 19 years; and at 74 only 11 years. You may have already beaten some of the pitfalls and land-mines of life that cause cognitive damage, along with those that will cause premature death. At age 55, fully one out of 10 of your birth year peers is already on the other side of the sod, at 65 nearly two out of 10, and at age 80 nearly half (46 percent) are already deceased. So, if the quantity of our days is left to our creator's choice, then what is left to our own choice? Our choice relevant to each day we are alive is the quality of that day; how we will live it. Spending whatever cash (not credit) is necessary on yourself and your spouse to meet that quality goal for the day should be done without guilt, regardless of what your inner self-critic, parents, peers, children, or extended family members try to force or encourage you to do financially.

Living a quality life for those days and years you may have remaining will require spending some money. Whatever your source of disposable income is, retirement is a time to spend it on yourself and spouse without reservation or much hesitation. Make your tithe to your church or synagogue if you do, and carefully and thoughtfully spend the rest to enjoy each day of the rest of your life.

To spend guiltlessly there is another acid test a spending choice must pass: the spending must be innocent. That is, the spending must be free of malice toward others and not used for the control of others. Your spending must be innocent of ill intent, crime, or wrongdoing of any kind. Money should never be spent to compromise your virtue or the virtue of others.

"Spend" means to disburse, use up, or consume. Many retired couples I've met have had divergent ideas about what to do with their accumulated wealth or monthly cash flows. They would say things that are clichés but do express true feelings like, "I want to spend my last dollar with my last breath" and the other spouse might say "I want to give all of my money when I die to the local humane society chapter." These very divergent opinions can lead to less than truly happy retired lives together. Similarly, I have met other couples who spend time trying to convince the other that their own idea for disposal of the joint estate's resources is the best plan. When one person of the retired couple is wishing to give resources away and the other person is paying worry and interest on future problems that do not yet exist, there is little room for compromise. Similarly, when one of the pair is wishing to give specific amounts to a few close people or family members and desires to give the remaining balance to the other spouse's charities, there is too much room for disagreement. The alternate spouse might be arguing for spending to enjoy life while they still have life and health and leaving anything that remains as a percentage split to the people and charities of choice. Whatever the finance-based impediments are to getting out there and enjoying retirement, they must be dealt with and, I dare say, dealt with first. Financial resources and how they will be used are a significant determinant relating to the quality of retirement for any couple.

The reality is that, in all probability, one spouse will die before the other, and any agreements about estate distribution can go null and void in one last heartbeat. There is a better way. If any of this strikes a chord as some of the things that are preventing you and your life partner from living and loving retirement on the same page, there is another option. Gifting to others, whatever the gift, is best enjoyed when you get to see the recipient unwrap it. Give now, and let it go—after all, it was a gift. A gift with no strings is easier on the giver and the receiver. Disburse to the charities and the people you care about while you are alive, of sound mind and body, and able to appreciate the results of your generous gifting. The recent TV show depicting rich volunteers provides a great example of gifting with feeling. At the end of each show, they write large checks to the charitable organizations they volunteered with. Give away what you must now, and spend the rest of what you earned and saved for your own benefit and enjoyment. By doing so, you can see the results firsthand of your philanthropy and free yourself of the worry of what will happen to assets after you die. By allowing yourself to enjoy the benefits of spending some of your resources generously on yourself, it can feel like giving a gift to yourself. Some feel that it is a doubly rewarding experience to gift to others, with the joy of giving and receiving in the same instant.

Avoid Excessive Use of Credit

I heard one woman say, "Sure, let's buy the half-million dollar motorhome. We will never live long enough to pay it off anyway." Taking on excessive debt as a retiree may be necessary in some circumstances where there is no other way to solve a serious problem. Taking on frivolous debt will rob you of future income and may add stress to what could otherwise be a stress-free lifestyle. The problem with large credit balances for retired individuals and couples is that it eliminates many of your future financial choices.

Depression-Era (pre-baby boom) retirees have a greater appreciation for paying for things with cash or doing without. Adjusting to a fixed income in retirement may be difficult, but I assure you using excessive credit does not fix the problem. The payment of interest is money wasted, and large payments are a bandit taking future choice away. It may be necessary to use credit for large purchases such as housing, automobiles, or recreational vehicle purchases, but using it for expensive vacations, daily living expenses, or frivolous purchases at the mall will lead to minimizing your future options and may bring huge regrets.

Minimize, Downsize, and Cast Off Things and the Worries that Can Go with Excessive Possessions

Another problem facing many retirees is what to do with their things. "What will happen to my things when I die?" is the question often articulated. The solution to that is simple, but hard for some to implement: become a practicing minimalist. To live a minimalist lifestyle, the fewer pieces of real estate, cars, toys, and possessions of all kinds that you have, the less energy and cash flow you will invest in worry, maintenance, insurance, repair, and upkeep. What you do not have will take no time, energy, and resources in upkeep or care. It truly is impossible to enjoy a home on the lake or in the woods when you are a thousand miles away and only spend a week or two there. Having a hundred pairs of shoes, Coach or Dooney & Bourke purses, or hundreds of collector hunting rifles does not make you a better person, and if those things or things like them bring you happiness, this book is probably wasted on you. It is the people you love and who will love you back and not things that should and will push the personal happiness meter well into the green at any time in your life, not only in retirement. Excessive possessions will not bring you true happiness. By holding things dear, things essentially begin to possess you; you become a slave to their upkeep and maintenance. If caught in this trap, consider gifting away or selling your excess possessions. There is a similar lesson in the Bible; the quote says that "it will be easier for a camel to go through the eye of a needle than for a rich man to enter the kingdom of God." In the Bible, the conflict is between trusting things or trusting the grace-filled promises of God's own redeeming work. In life, over-embracing things (or money) prevents one from trusting your own ability to find inner peace and work toward achieving personal happiness in the daily pursuit of truly living out your life in meaningful ways.

A recent TV ad by a major financial and insurance company stated that the average retiree has 6,000 sunsets or sunrises to look forward to, or about 16 years. The question is this: with an average of only 6,000 more sunrises to look forward to, how many hours of those days do you want to consume with financial issues or asset care, security, and maintenance concerns about property and possessions. Every hour spent on worry or concern over your possessions could restrain the enjoyment of your remaining days.

To twist another financial company's TV ad just a bit remember "It's your money, and you can spend it now." Feel free to spend it your way; you earned it, right along with the right to choose how to use it.

CHAPTER 2

Exercising Control

There are way too many things that can get under your skin and into your head with thoughts that will start to tug at your behavior as if you were a marionette on string. From birth on, as humans, we are constantly being manipulated by others, beginning with our parents, our older siblings, and others in authority. In our early years of development, much of that is necessary for our survival and our overall well-being. Moving from home to school, we were conditioned to follow the rules: some useful, some particularly stupid. Regardless of the school rules' efficacy, follow them we must, as we are taught from an early age to do so. Many of us were bullied by upperclassmen and stronger peers. Religion and its taboos, and for some the lack of religion in one's life, tend to dampen what might otherwise be an opportunity for you to become free to be yourself.

Unfortunately, this early conditioning makes us all too susceptible to living a life of moving from one source of control to the next. From our parents to school to church to the boss at work to spouses—and the list potentially goes on and on, with us having little to say about what we want of life let alone getting it. It is akin to being given a brand-new red convertible and always having to ride in the passenger seat.

As adults out in the world and living in neighborhoods, there is a change in who tries and succeeds at manipulating our behavior. Community and neighborhood pressures influence people in two ways. One is internal and is expressed by the clichés "keeping up with the Joneses" or apprehensive thoughts of "what will the neighbor's think?" The other is in the form of neighborhood associations that exert pressure for conformance. These are two of the more recognizable community pressures. Others are less in-your-face and include perceived community values, community mores, and community gossip. Our own children as they grow up often move from being influenced by us to being an influence on us as we age to elderly. This control over aging parents can reach a peak when you are considering your retirement options and are making decisions that will influence your retired lifestyle, and your children object.

Certainly, we still have to behave and operate in a system in which respect for and compliance with the law is maintained. Running afoul of the law will have consequences and can ruin a retirement plan unlike anything else. The laws of our land are not what we are talking about setting aside here. The law is the law, and it must be complied with or one risks the perils and consequences of being adjudicated a law breaker.

Setting External Influences Aside

As adults, as retired adults in particular, the unwelcome influences we consciously and unconsciously pay attention to, subtle and not so subtle, all of the things and people working to control us to our own spirit's detriment, must be put aside. The freedom to decide, to make choices is not just a political virtue; it is truly an individual virtue as well. Whatever it might be that is coming at us to take away our choices from outside sources must be put aside and behind you in retirement: do not let external influences run or ruin your remaining life. This is the time in your life where it is not only OK, it is necessary to get in the driver's seat and take over the controls.

Opposing Those Contrary Voices

I was amused when one of my 62-year-old friends related to me all the things her older sister cautioned her about before she left her sister's house to come and visit me. My friend thought that, at her age, she had successfully managed thousands of visits to friends and acquaintances and really did not need the behavioral advice from an older sister. The truth is she did not need it and was mature enough to recognize that she did not need it. Even mature enough to tell me about it and joke about it. Taking this approach and realizing that her sister could not stop being a pseudo-parent, yet doing as she wanted anyway was a healthy adult choice.

The two lessons here are that (1) it is time to let go of the reins you use you try to exercise control over others and (2) to remove their bit from your own mouth as well. Regardless of the source of those opposing voices—be they children, friends, family, extended family, neighbors, or in some cases the professionals you hire or engage with—set these external influences under your own control, subordinate them to your own reason and intelligent choice. People all too often feel it is necessary to comply with influences from "friends"; this often forces us to think that we must do this or that or live in a certain way to "fit in" with the group or relationship. Readers, you are adults now, probably over 50, you are old enough to make your own choices: give yourself complete permission to do so.

Habit two is one many of us think we own but not everyone does to the extent necessary to achieve happiness. Be honest with yourself in your analysis of the degree you practice this habit.

Happily Retired Habit #2

Always pull your own strings.

———————

Stated another way, have the courage to run your own show. Set yourself free in order to experience the total freedom of conscious choice, maybe for the first time in your life. Revel in the power you feel over your life in the daily choices you make. This habit alone has the power to bring you to a new destiny in retirement. We are not talking about being or becoming selfish and self-centered and entirely ignoring the needs of others. What I am referring to here is to simply know within yourself that you are a true adult and that it is more than OK to make your own decisions; it is absolutely necessary to do so. I am not suggesting total rebellion against everything and everyone here. I am suggesting that it is more than OK and totally adult to say *yes* to something only when you mean it and want to say yes and to say *no* to any suggestion, proposal, or command when it just doesn't feel right for you at the time. It is also the honest thing to do.

Also avoid letting anything you would consider a vice control your life in retirement. There are many things that can ruin the quality of a person's retirement. Excessive alcohol consumption, legal or illegal drug dependency, being a shopaholic, and having a gambling addiction are a just a handful of the social behaviors that, alone or together, will rob you of a quality retirement and rob you of the complete control of being yourself and achieving your retirement destiny.

Some readers might have problems with setting aside certain overly restrictive religious influences. All too often, religion can play a negative role in controlling the decisions people make. There are two aspects to think about on this topic. The first one is that of religious freedom itself as a matter of law. In the United States, we consider as a fundamental right the freedom to practice any religion of our choice within the bounds of the rest of our body of law. Essentially, we are free to practice a religion provided that religion is not harmful to ourselves or others. This civil freedom also provides an out to practice no religion at all. The second aspect to consider—and one not well understood—is the potential to live your life in the *freedom provided by your religion*. Beyond the basics restrictions on bad behavior that most all religions espouse, some prohibitions offered up by certain religions such as prohibitions on hair length, the wearing of jewelry, associations with others outside of the congregation, or even the teaching that good works are necessary for salvation could all be things that have no impact on one's eternal salvation. For example a concept of freedom preached by Lutheran Christian denominations allows believers to revel in the freedom to live one's life, with access to heaven provided solely by a trusting faith in Christ's atoning work of salvation. Every seat in the Christian church worldwide is at least in theory one provided for a sinner on Sunday morning by a grace filled God.

Freedom to choose one's activities and actions in life, as long as those activities and actions are not harmful to yourself or others, is the definition of freedom. The United States Declaration of Independence includes the phrase "liberty and the pursuit of happiness." This phrase is cast in law for you, and the time to exercise that freedom is now.

Whatever strings that are attached to you that rob you of your self-control, and ultimately your self-respect, must be set aside to live a life of your own choosing in retirement.

CHAPTER 3

Living Those Dreams

President Reagan's famous quote (originally attributed to Hillel the Elder) comes to mind here. He said something close to: "If not us, who? And if not now when?" In all probability, now that you are retired, you have already lived more years than you will have left to live. I have yet to meet an adult who does not have some thoughts or dreams about how he or she would like to spend his or her time once retired. Wasting away in Margaritaville or any other "ville" is not the concept for this habit. This habit of seemingly happy retired people is all about getting up, getting out, and getting going.

Happily Retired Habit #3

Have a bucket list and act on it.

I was always a busy dad when my boys were growing up. Probably did not spend anywhere near enough time with them. I remember one day when my youngest son was in his early teens, and we were sitting in a fast food pal-

ace having a burger and fries. That day was one set aside
for being with him. I asked him "What would you like to
do today?" His reply was "Go fly a kite." Not sure how to
take his reply, I was taken aback for a few seconds. After
thinking about it to myself for a few seconds, I asked "why
not?" So I said "OK, let's go!" We went to the kite shop at
the airport a few miles away, brought the new giant kite
kit home to our acreage, and had a great day taking turns
flying a very cool new box kite. It was one of our better
days together. Grant yourself the freedom to follow these
kinds of impulses. There is no reason to say no to yourself
when it comes to following reasonably safe pursuits, no
matter how fantastic, outlandish, or out of character they
may seem to others. Walk the Appalachian Trail. Learn to
play the harmonica. Go for the hot-air balloon ride. Take
a tandem sky dive. Go on that Mediterranean cruise. Drive
the ALCAN Highway to Alaska. Get a massage. Go to the
spa. Take that Canadian fishing trip. Drive your F150 to
the Panama Canal. Pedal bike across your town, county,
or state or from New York to LA. Go to New York and
see a Broadway play. Whatever is on your lifelong "I wish
I could do list," retirement is the time to get going and
check off a few items on your bucket list as "completed."

Whatever time you have remaining, this is your time:
use it. Now is the time for you to be yourself. You got to
this point in time; you have earned the right to follow your
own fanciful pursuits and interests. The time is now to
do all or as many of the things you set aside and deferred

for "someday" or "retirement." It is time to do all of those things that you promised yourself you would do "maybe someday." Every day of retirement is a "someday" to follow those dreams and lifelong desires.

If you have not seen the movie, a *bucket list* is a sheet(s) of paper where you write down all of the things, people, events, and places you want to do *before you die*. Married couples, please cooperate here: both spouses (partners) must have a bucket list. Trade off one for one or come up with a plan where you both get to check off things on your lists. Use some give and take, and share the use of resources as equally as possible when it comes to achieving the check boxes marked on the bucket lists as completed. If you really want to grow older together, cooperation on the "want to do" list has to be the key to mutual happiness. If necessary, establish three lists, a "mine," "yours," and "ours" list of retirement endeavors. The "ours" list for a couple should hopefully be the longest list.

All too often, when talking to widows and widowers, I hear them say things like "We really wanted to visit the Grand Canyon and Hoover Dam, but Chuck died last year and now we'll never get the chance." Take control and act on the list today to avoid these unwanted regrets. If you have not written down a list of things you have always wanted to do, do it now. Without getting too detailed, write out your own *to do before you die* list. Estimate the cost, and put that on the sheet along with a proposed date for getting that item checked off. Doing so will move you closer to getting them done and focused on what it will take to achieve success for each item on your list. The bottom line is that retirement is not only a time to enjoy good memories from the past, it is time to make some totally new memories for your future years. If there is anything that you have always wanted to do but have not had the chance—assuming it is legal, moral, and just—it belongs on the list.

Expect that others will say "You're going to do what??!!" That is OK to hear; odds are they are probably stifling their own dreams, too. Feel free to ignore the negative commentary and press ahead when you have achieved those goals—those same people will be jealous of you. It's not OK for you to opt out of living to the fullest just to please someone else. It's your bucket list, you can do it. Let naysayers hammer out or hammer on their own lists. This bucket list is yours, thank you very much. Your list to do whatever you please, beginning any day you please.

Today's actions are the building material for tomorrow's memories. No matter your condition, age, or heath, there are some things you can do today that will store up more precious memories for tomorrow. With any luck at all, you will always be too busy building new adventures and accomplishments to have time to dwell on past memories.

CHAPTER 4

Discover and Unleash Your Inner Creativity

Throughout our working lives, most of us were engaged and encouraged to engage in what is considered "left-brain activities." Even for the creative types, parts of the jobs required application of logic, routine, math skills, and engaging in activities considered routine and often absent of creativity. Regardless of how we feel about ourselves, each of us has a creative side. All too often throughout our working lives and because of demands on our time with work, family, and social responsibilities, our personal creativity is set aside to handle the daily problems, challenges, and issues of living, working, and bringing up a family in a modern society.

It is sad when this stifled creative genius in each of us is shunted aside by the demands of daily living. Whatever is keeping your creative side suppressed, it is important to find a way to deal with the problem. Avoid passing into eternity with all of the proverbial music (fun and personally rewarding activities) still stuck inside of you. Let it out. Let it be you. If you have ever uttered any of these next three sentences, you will immediately understand this fourth habit.

"I have always wanted to _____."

"I'd like to try ____ sometime."

"Never done ____ but it might be fun to try it once."

I was spending some time in a nursing home with a loved one who was approaching her 103rd birthday. I asked her what she would have done differently in her life or what she regretted the most. She related to me a time when she was a very young child and her parents were financially challenged. She wanted a toy piano, a Shoenhut wooden baby grand piano with eight white keys and five black keys so she could learn to key out some music. She never got the piano and never pursued music. It was a sad memory in what was otherwise a vibrant and vital life.

Unachieved creative goals are always regrettable. Fill in the blank spaces in the three sentences above with whatever unique creative activity fits you and your dreams. Perhaps you have always wanted to act in a theater or maybe cast a statue in bronze. Whatever creative pursuit you have put on hold, retirement is the time to answer that call to get moving toward some unfulfilled creative outlet.

Happily Retired Habit #4

Write, sing, paint, perform, or play.

Those people who have been able to pursue careers and develop their creative side as well as meet their logical career-developing demands are truly fortunate. Throughout so much of our working lives, most of us have been focused on left-brain logical activities. We have found little time outside of work for making the artistic and more creative activities and energies inside of us come out in productive, rewarding, and entertaining ways. Maybe you have never ventured to this side of your brain or taken chances with creative pursuits or playing at something because others (teachers are famous for this) always "put you down" or criticized past attempts at unleashing your creative side. Let's face it, first learning to play the trombone is rarely a pretty sound. Having to color between the lines is great if you were intent on becoming an engineer—not so much if you were a budding Picasso.

Creative talents must often be expressed by "coloring outside of the lines." Prehistoric men and women found time to paint on their cave walls and cave ceilings to tell their story; there is no reason for you to feel restrained from figuratively doing the same thing. Tell the tale of your creativity by acting on those unfulfilled creative desires. Quit talking about it and write that book. Join the city band, choir, or the local harmony quartet. Build birdhouses, learn to paint, learn to sew or knit, join a community theater group: whatever it is that you have held in check all this time. Take the time to at least give a new hobby a try.

It's best that you be the sole judge of your creative talents, not anyone from your past or present. Become your own critic until you are ready to showcase your new talent to all. Trying new creative pursuits and failing miserably is far more rewarding than keeping the desire bottled up inside.

Work to overcome the natural barriers to unleashing your creativity. The first barrier is your own self-critic. Silence that inner critic by accepting that mistakes will be made and that perfection is a pursuit—not a component—of every creative work. Every painting is training for the next canvas. Let your creative mind find its way off the shelf you may have kept it on. Another obstacle that may need to be overcome is that of knowledge or skill. A new creative endeavor may require some practice, reading, research, or classes, all of which can add depth to your creative journey. Finally, unleash the motivation to follow through. Even if it feels like work at first, a first successful creation or performance will provide its own unique rewards.

CHAPTER 5

Deal with Your Mortality

Some say "I have had a good life and, if I die tomorrow, that's OK." Those charged with taking care of your final needs and your estate may not feel the same way. There is no time to waste. Time is not on your side on this issue. Personal procrastination will not make this problem go away. You will die at some point, there are many things that need to be dealt with, and you are the best person to deal with planning for your final requests.

Happily Retired Habit #5

Have your final plans dealt with.

Your death is going to be traumatic enough to those who love you. Don't make it worse for them by dumping bigger problems on them than is necessary when you finally meet your earthly demise.

Bequeath while you are still alive, giving yourself the benefit of seeing the value of your gifts. Make your wishes known by planning your own funeral and documenting

your desires. Talk to your pastor, priest, rabbi, or offici-
ating clergy. Plan your funeral out, and write down your
instructions to include every detail that matters, even
down to who will cater the luncheon after your interment.
Make a complete plan on how you would like your funeral
or memorial service to go and write it down. Let a few of
your family members or friends in on where to find the
information, and let them in on as many of the details as
you feel they need to know now. Talk to your clergy person
and go over with them those things that will be important
for you and then write them down, too. Keep this funeral/
religious service outline with your important legal papers
and insurance policies. Make sure some trusted person
knows where to find these papers.

Take or select the picture to go with your obituary.
Write out your draft obituary. Write out what you would
like to appear in your obituary and which newspapers you
would like it to appear in. Let your executor and next of
kin hold a copy of it, and keep another copy in with your
important papers.

If you feel it necessary, you can go the next step and
actually prearrange and prepay for you funeral service by
using a reputable funeral parlor that offers prepaid plans.
Communicate with a trusted funeral director and pick
out your coffin, determine your final resting place, and
the elements desired for any visitation or special graveside
ceremony. Prepay for this service or bank final expenses
or fund them with life insurance. Let your executor know

what you have done by final letter or in a conversation ahead of time.

You should face your own inevitable demise and deal with these things to make things easier on your loved ones and family. I remember when my favorite aunt, one of my mother's sisters—actually, I suppose she was everybody's favorite aunt—was facing major heart surgery. It was iffy surgery, she was told of the risks, but decided to go ahead with it anyway. She was reconciled to the idea that if the surgery was successful she would get an additional portion of quality time here on Earth to be with family and friends. She was asked prior to the surgery by a close friend who was afraid of the whole proposition "What will happen if you die?" Without a moment's hesitation she said "My friends will miss me." As a Christian she trusted the promise of salvation for all those who confess that Jesus work of redemption is achieved in everyone willing to receive and open the gift of God's saving grace with a thankful heart. Her surgery did not work out, and we all miss her while remembering her great example of faith in facing her own mortality. She died within days after the procedure. We do all miss her and so do her friends. Those who love you will miss you, too. Help them out by finding a way to let them know what your final wishes are.

Taking this action reduces the burden on the loved ones you will leave behind. Even if you have no close family members left, your friends or executor will be much less stressed if they know what your final wishes are. Allow them enough information to do the job the way you would want it done.

- ❏ Make a will (if needed).
- ❏ Plan your funeral and visitation service.
- ❏ Fund your final expenses.
- ❏ Plan your memorial/religious service.
- ❏ Write a draft obituary.
- ❏ Select (and purchase if needed) your final resting place.

Tell your executor, clergy, and next of kin where these plan documents can be found, and tell them as much as you feel comfortable telling them now. They do not need to know every detail or any details if that is your choice, but some trusted others do need to know where to find the information.

You only have to make this plan once and maybe check it over every couple of years to make sure the plan still reflects your wishes and maintains the continuity needed for your loved ones. This habit is a one-time thing in the doing, yet it provides everyday peace of mind in the knowing that it has been done.

CHAPTER 6

Live the Rest of Your Life with a Clear Conscience

Some lives are lived in ways that cause one to accumulate a catalog of past regrets. We all have some regrets. Opportunities not capitalized or tried, roads not taken, wrong turns, relationships gone wrong, missed investments . . . the lists can just keep on getting longer with each passing year. The regrets that matter and haunt people most during the down times in retirement are those where we have consciously or unconsciously wronged someone else or hurt someone close, seemingly beyond repair. Those circumstances that hurt us equally are ones where we have been wronged by a family member or someone we felt a genuine love toward or closeness with. To fully enjoy your retirement days, it is necessary to rid your conscience of current and past regrets. You must take the steps necessary to unburden your spirit.

Begin by Repairing Unresolved Relationships

One of the best pieces of advice and example I have found is to grant forgiveness without any reservation and to seek forgiveness relentlessly. Grant to others your forgiveness, no matter how much they have hurt you in the past. Unresolved is not solved in any way. Push in to those who have pulled away to reach a conclusion to the past relationship issues. Sometimes that conclusion, after all of your best efforts to mend fences and find forgiveness from someone, is simply to "forgive them for not forgiving you" and move on with your life without them in it in any way. To do that successfully, you have to ask for forgiveness more than once and do so with the utmost sincerity.

As you continue to age, the regrets that will haunt you the most will not be the ones involving money, or career, or spending decisions. As time passes, you will most likely lose sleep and deeply suffer remorse from formerly close relationships gone wrong and not resolved, and, worse, by not having taken some time and energy toward attempting to fix the issues. There are two distinct groups: one is problems and offenses you have committed toward others, and the second is those wrongs that have been committed against you that have been particularly hurtful. Often, we hurt or are hurt by family members or people who are really close to us. This emotional baggage, the kind that will often bring tears to one's eyes just thinking about them, are the ones I am talking about here. In some cases, the people we have wronged or who have wronged us are already dead, making us feel helpless about fixing the relationship. Harboring hate for anyone deceased only hurts our own psyche. Expecting the deceased to come back and apologize to us is not likely to happen either.

Often, failed family relationships are not resolved before the death of one of the parties, which makes repairing the relationship impossible. In order for you to extricate yourself from the potential for this very sad trap, you must take the first step to right the relationships without delay. You must act, now. Live your retirement without regrets by engaging in habit number six.

Happily Retired Habit #6

*Relentlessly forgive others and likewise
seek forgiveness from others.*

I wish I would have. . . . If only I would have said. . . . If only I could take that back I would. . . . If things had been different. . . . These are sayings and feelings that should slip away forever. If the injured party or the person showing you malice does not reciprocate in kind, it is now on them. Cleanse your own conscience and move on. This only works if you invest the time and energy that it takes to actually ask for forgiveness first when necessary and take the steps necessary to let others know you have forgiven them.

If you find moving on difficult, be mindful that Christian doctrine teaches that sin will not be accounted against one who is contrite and in faith accepts that Christ accomplished his saving work for all through his own sacrifice. Whether you are a person of faith does not immediately matter in personal relationships gone wrong. What matters immediately is that you forgive those who have wronged you and that you let those who are still alive know that you have forgiven them, regardless of whether they ask for forgiveness or not. *Don't carry the hate in your heart; let it go and let them know.*

I am told that my father often said and lived by the biblical statement found in Paul's letters to the Ephesians to "never let the sun set on a grudge." If days, months, or even years have passed on damaged relationships, as long as both parties are alive, there is still time to ask for and grant forgiveness for the wrongdoings, mistakes, and misunderstandings. This will not happen without someone taking the necessary steps, meaning you are the one who has to take responsibility.

For those you have offended, relentlessly seek them out and actively, clearly, and sincerely ask for their forgiveness. If they are not ready to grant it, even though you have asked, your part is done and you can move on with a clear conscience. The burden of harboring hate in the heart and soul becomes theirs alone at that point. The consequences to you when others wronged you will not necessarily go away, nor will the consequences of your hurting others; however, the hurt will not renew itself every day of your life if you seek and grant forgiveness.

One more thing: everyone makes decisions that they are not particularly proud of, so forgive your self, too. For those mistakes you have stubbornly made that caused problems and undesirable consequences in your own life, right now, this minute say to yourself: "_____ (*your name*) I forgive you for all the things you've done that were not quite right. I am sorry, I did not mean to hurt you! Forgive me now." Then add: "_____ (*your name*) I forgive you!"

When you are free of the burdens of past mistakes, you are free to move on optimistically with the rest of your life with a cheerful heart. You will probably go on and continue to make occasional relationship mistakes as you live your life. The habit of forgiveness is one to exercise and use as often as needed; every day if necessary. Harmony and quality in your retired life will be much easier to achieve when you own the habit of forgiveness.

On the other side of the forgiveness coin is hatred. As a retiree, there should be little time or energy wasted on hate toward anyone, any entity, government, group, or anything else. Some retirees are so busy hating the president and congress, the neighbor across the street, an old coworker, or what a bad job their parents did at raising them, it is hard to be in the same space with them for very long because they can't stop telling you who, what, and how much they hate. This trap that some people are stuck in only serves to make them and anyone who comes in contact with them miserable if not completely nauseated. Your golf partner does not really care if you hate the president or who you didn't vote for. He or she might actually appreciate a golf tip or two. In every election, one side wins the other loses; that is just how it goes. Get over it. No one wants to be around or hear endless negative commentary unless they, too, have a mental problem already. When a person harbors the habit of forgiveness in his or her life, it permeates his or her thinking about all aspects of life, and as one forgives, it allows one to move on to doing something with the positive potential in life. Dwelling in the cesspool of hate is indeed a stinky way to live. The energy wasted on negativism could be so much better spent on creative endeavors and building others up. If, after an honest accounting, you find you are a Negative Ned or Nellie, stop the behavior now and start focusing on building the habit of forgiveness into your life.

CHAPTER 7

Practice Some Form of Philanthropy

The seventh habit is a very simple one that can be done with or without any financial resources at your disposal.

Happily Retired Habit #7

Give something of yourself to others.

———

Our creator's desire is that beyond our gifts of love back to him, we should share our time, talent, and treasures and be examples of love in this world. We hear it in many clichés: paying forward, giving back, payback, random acts of kindness; regardless of your religious philosophy, it is the right thing to do. Even if you are not a religious person by nature or upbringing, you should be able to appreciate the concept of being sufficiently unselfish enough to cheerfully give something of yourself to others. The help unselfishly rendered to others will do wonders for you in return. It is easy to share those things that we have plenty of, those things we would not miss. Sharing a few apples or even a bushel off of a full tree is too easy, and that is not the kind of unselfish giving I am presenting here. Perhaps turning that equation around, keeping a few apples for your own use and giving the rest of the tree's output to others would be a little closer to the idea. What I am saying is to give to others enough so that it hurts at least a little bit, if only for a minute or two. Apples, of course, are a metaphor for whatever it is that you have of value to share with others who do not possess what you can share. Let me give you an example from my own experience.

One summer, my wife and I volunteered at a Christian camp for 107 days. For starters, that is nearly 30 percent of a year. It is a long time to put your own life on hold to give time and your life's energy to others on a daily basis. We were not fond of the management after being there for only a few weeks, the board of directors was composed of less-than-stellar leaders, and some of the board members' spouses were downright mean-spirited. We had only six hours off twice during our tenure there, and we felt like we worked way too hard most days. Needless to say, when it was time to go, we were very much ready to go. It was work, real hard work, and we were tired, you might even say even to the point of being spent. There was, however, an upside, a huge upside that we did not anticipate on the front-end of our time there. First of all, we learned a lot about the inner workings of a Christian camp, what is necessary financially, and the various skilled manual labors needed to keep such a place going. Learning anything is always worth something. Next, we were able to help people in need directly, in meaningful ways, during our stay. We made a lasting physical difference by improving the facilities with our daily labor and expended mechanical skills. Most importantly, though, we met and became acquainted with some very admirable young people who will be leaders in their fields of study, their communities, and community churches. Some of them we now count as friends and are anxious to see them continue their journey past college and into the work-a-day world and to see them establish families of their own. Money can't buy any of that. Sitting home can't either. We will do it again; just not there and not real soon! There are so many other things that need doing, we're sure to find something. After the first month, staying at that camp became harder every day, but stay we did. Giving of that time and service was a bit painful but, surprisingly, equally rewarding.

Your gift to share might be time, talent, treasure, or knowledge. What it is does not matter all that much. The fact that you are willing and able to share—and to share often—does matter. The fact that you are filling some real need in society matters as well. We have met many retired couples who have volunteered in strange places after natural disasters or who go on congregation- or organization-sponsored trips to build housing or places of worship, and many others who do so every few years. You can tell the difference when meeting and talking with those who find the ability to periodically give of themselves to others and those who do not have the experience. The apparent givers seem happier than those who don't. It is that simple.

As I said in the Introduction, my credentials for writing this book include the fact that I have lived a while and never wasted an opportunity to observe and digest inferences from the experience and examples of others. One simply does not have the time or inclination to experience everything in one's own lifetime. We must learn from freely observing the experiences of others. If you have not already found a way to give of yourself in and as a part of your retirement, try something out and see how you feel about it after the deed is done. See the box for a few ideas you may find nearby, no matter where you live.

Action Ideas

- ❏ Knit for a child care nursery.
- ❏ Work as a server in a community soup kitchen.
- ❏ Collect food or distribute food for the community pantry of food bank.
- ❏ Volunteer at a community shelter.
- ❏ Volunteer at a VA or community hospital.
- ❏ Work at a crisis center.
- ❏ Support an abused women's' shelter.
- ❏ Become a mentor.

Today, there is no shortage of people in need; what we are short of is people willing and able to meet those needs in meaningful ways. The most significant ways to contribute are those that, over time, eliminate the others' need for help entirely. Teaching general job skills, coaching life skills, tutoring students in math or language skills, or running writing or art seminars are a few things that can turn people with needs into people with the ability to contribute to others.

Give something of value to others, give it cheerfully, and give it often. Appreciate nothing more than a thank you in return and say to the receiver(s) "Happy to help!" and mean it.

Find a need, find a niche where you can make a difference, and begin your personal adventure in charitable giving of yourself to others today.

CHAPTER 8

Nurture Your Best Existing Habits

If you have done little more in getting to retirement than avoiding the pitfalls and land mines of life you have, to a great extent, already acquired many habits of successful people on your own. Retirement is not the time to throw off the good habits that have proved beneficial to living well. There are three areas to hold fast to; these are good habits and behaviors you already own that contribute to the heath of your body, the exercise of your mind, and the nurturing of your soul.

Give Yourself Due Credit for the Things You Are Already Doing Right

Avoid giving up on doing what you consider to be good in your life, regardless of your chronological age. Getting to the point of seeking increased quality in a retired lifestyle suggests that you are probably already in possession of some very beneficial existing habits. Working on self-improvement and getting regular exercise are examples of good habits that are frequently held by all retirees. Doing some self-maintenance or self-improvement activities that have served you well in the past regularly in retirement is a positive activity. But since you have purchased this book and read it to this point, you must have recognized a need to find something more for yourself. The reason to buy this book could be that you do not feel happy or fulfilled facing or experiencing your retirement. This tells me that your current good habits might not be well-rounded. Now that retirement has freed you from the time burdens of work, self-maintenance and self-improvement activities should move to the forefront of your daily agenda. Along with self-maintenance activities, devote some time daily to embracing new self-improvement activities. Both of these are habits most retires already own to some degree or another, so all that is necessary in retirement is to hold on to these current habits that are good and beneficial and improve on them if necessary. Continue to care for and improve the "three wheels" that propel you into a happy and rewarding retirement: your body, mind, and spirit. Use the information presented in the next few sections to check on how you are progressing in retirement with positive actions.

Continue the Systematic Care and Feeding of Your Body

Maintaining one's good health is a priority in retirement. It is difficult to follow through and accomplish retirement goals and objectives without staying as healthy as is individually possible.

Action Ideas

- ❏ Eat healthy, well-balanced meals in moderation.
- ❏ Submit to an annual physical examination by your doctor or primary medical care provider.
- ❏ Get regular dental checkups and professional teeth cleanings.
- ❏ Maintain all necessary medications and diet regimens.
- ❏ Engage in moderate but regular exercise. Fifteen to 20 minutes twice a day is said to be sufficient.
- ❏ Maintain personal hygiene. If your health status and budget will allow it, treat yourself to the "extras" like spa treatments, periodic massages, or time in the hot tub.
- ❏ Avoid harmful excesses of all sorts. Examples of things to avoid include overeating, too much alcohol, overmedication, inactivity, gambling, excessive exercise, unprotected sex with strangers, or illegal drugs.

Every Day, Find One or More Ways to Challenge Your Mind

Depression and despair can be exacerbated by the mind's inactivity. Find something challenging that you like to do.

Find at least one activity that you can do alone and some that you can do with your spouse, company, or friends.

Action Ideas

- ❏ Read.
- ❏ Do cross-word and math puzzles.
- ❏ Play solitaire and other card games.
- ❏ Build puzzles.
- ❏ Take college classes; sometimes free to senior citizens at major state-funded universities as audit classes.
- ❏ Play video games.
- ❏ Learn a new language.
- ❏ View educational television programming.

Maintain Your Spiritual Health

Take the steps necessary to maintain your spiritual health. The human spirit occupies the space in our minds between our logical mind and our eternal soul. Whether you are willing to acknowledge it or not, you have a soul; perhaps it is truer that we are really spiritual souls that occupy physical bodies for a period of time. Each one of us does have a natural awareness of the potential for an eternal spirit world. There is a feeling that something in you will survive your body's physical death. For those who wish to deny the existence of a spiritual purpose in our lives and the existence of a God, I would submit to you two thoughts. First, that the activities associated with denying the existence of God becomes your religion. Second, that it takes more faith to believe that pure chance leads to the proper collection and assembly of primordial atoms into your thinking, feeling, and emotional body than it does to acknowledge that there is a powerful hand at work here that we do not and cannot ever fully understand. Think of this for a minute. Everything that makes you—the basic building blocks of the atoms, minerals, chemicals, electrical energy, and every other component of the human body—as present at the big bang or whenever the universe and our planetary system came into being. The assembly of all those components into a living, breathing, thinking, and feeling human being is not just another accident. There is a reason you are here on this earth at this place and in this time. We don't yet fully understand DNA, but it fashions each and every one of us into unique beings. We don't fully understand what comprises our soul and its purpose, but its role in our living purpose-filled lives is no less important than the role DNA plays in shaping our bodies.

Action Ideas

❑ Pray.
❑ Go to religious services.

❏ Read sacred texts.
❏ Attend a religious studies class.
❏ Seek out clergy for individual instruction.

CHAPTER 9

Live Large in the Present

$\mathbf{F}$ar too many retirees I have chatted with leave me with the impression that they truly believe their best days are behind them and that life will never be as good as it once was. As we age, there are inevitable changes in the pace of how our bodies continue to grow and regenerate. Our skin changes and ages, our hair loses its color, and the rush of energy we used to have evades us some days. We may not remember details like we used to. The inevitability of all of these changes and effects may be mostly out of your control. The one thing that we can control as we age is our choice of how we approach each remaining day of life. Every minute of your life is precious. Use each minute to live the life you want for yourself.

My "shirttail uncle" Chet retired the year I was born and lived to be 101 years old. He lived a solid 50 years of an independent, retired lifestyle before needing any help or care with the details of daily living. One of my mother's aunts who lived the last part of her life alone was also blessed with 100 plus years. My wife's mother lived past her 103rd birthday and was on NBC national news for being still able to bowl with an 18-pound bowling ball at age 100. I don't know for certain, but I would guess that if you asked any of these people at the point of their own retirement if their best days were behind them, I'd bet the answer would have been a solid "no way." The truth is that you have the responsibility for adjusting your attitude to be open to the idea and outlook that your very best days may be just around the corner and, at the very least, believing that some good days are still to come, regardless of your chronological age today.

Sure, you could be right; your very best days up to this point may have already passed you by. Some of the trouble signs to look for include too many statements to yourself or others that begin with "Remember when" or "I used to" or "Back when I was...." It is okay to look back from time to time, but consuming your day with backward-looking memories robs you of the time and opportunity to turn today into something special in its own right. If you live the rest of your days with the idea that your best days are already behind you, it will likely be a self-fulfilling prophesy denying the added pleasure and fulfillment that can be yours any day of your life. Instead, begin the rest of your retirement life with the idea, feeling, and sincere hope that good times can still be yours. Own that positive thinking with every fiber of your being.

Every day you wake up is a gift of time to be invested in something you value or something of value for yourself or to benefit others. Seize each dawning day and make the best use of it that is possible within your current circumstances and environment. Having had good times and good days in the past does not mean that you have filled your quota; there is no quota on good days or good times. You can have as many as you are willing to invest the days' time and energy into. Each sunrise and setting can bring enjoyment and happiness to those who are willing to accept, indeed expect, that today, this very day… will bring positive feelings simply because one is alive. Each day and the choices presented by each day's arrival are yours to make and enjoy.

To become a forward-looking instead of a backward-looking person, there is one very easy exercise to turn your thinking to in making the most of the future. At the end of each day or at the beginning of each new day, make out a list of what you wish to accomplish in the next 24 hours. Not a big list or a minute-by-minute list. Just set down one, two, or three things you want to accomplish to take advantage of this new day. In our house, my wife and I talk about it and share our lists with each other in terms of what we call big rocks and little rocks. An example might be "My big rock for today is taking you to lunch. And my little rocks are to pick up some new printer ink and paper while we are out."

Her reply might be "OK, as long as we are home by three so I can finish reading a chapter or two in my new book before I start on making supper." We share our big and little goals for the day no matter how gigantic or trivial they might be. The stress of being at cross purposes goes away, and the sharing also often leads to mutual support toward accomplishing our joint and independent goals for each new day.

Now that you have read this entire book, ask yourself this question: When someone meets you and verbally tells part of the story of your life to someone else, beginning with the sentence "Did you ever notice how _____ (*fill in your name here*) seems so very happy? I think it is because he/she_____(*fill in the blank*)!" What will others say about you? What would you say about yourself?

The choices and actions needed to lead a meaningful life in retirement are yours. Retirement is the opportunity for you to become the person you have always wanted to be. Try not to let the opportunity to live a cheerful retirement slip past you from inaction on your part.

Thanks for reading this—I hope it helps.

Dennis C. Brewer

Index

Index

Made in the USA
Columbia, SC
02 June 2022

61186240R00049